The Last Dealership

What needs to be done now to prevent the extinction of the great American dealership.

Aharon Horwitz

Eliav Moshe

Yishai Goldstein

Book cover by Mollie Monett **Illustrations** by Irena Ilyaev

Fullpath
The Last Dealership

All rights reserved
Copyright © 2024 by Fullpath

No part of this publication may be reproduced, distributed, or transmitted in any form or by any means, including photocopying, recording, or other electronic or mechanical methods, without the prior written permission of the publisher, except in the case of brief quotations embodied in critical reviews and certain other noncommercial uses permitted by copyright law.

Published by *Spines*
ISBN: 979-8-89383-075-0

CONTENTS

To our indomitable team who, be it through plague or strife, faithfully serve our customers day in and out.

To Andrew Walser, who taught us to "crawl, walk, run," and always encouraged us to innovate hard but deliver it "Fisher Price."

To the "Quirk Boys," Sean Western and Brandon Sweeney, who have no fear and elevate us to new levels every year.

INTRODUCTION

The three of us were not born "car guys," yet we built a Customer Data Platform (CDP) and a marketing automation platform (MAP) that now serve thousands of North American car dealerships, including some of the most savvy and forward leading auto-retailers in the United States. These dealerships have been our teachers and pathfinders as we've tried to bring our own special contribution to this incredible industry.

Our startup, Fullpath, was born of our passion for the impact that small, medium, and family-owned businesses have on local communities and economies. We feel that the very best way to preserve middle-class opportunity in the United States and other creativity-powered democratic economies – like Israel, where the three of us live – is by protecting, fostering, and strengthening businesses exactly like franchised auto-dealerships. These community-rooted businesses pay good wages, are accountable to local audiences, and offer a path to social and financial advancement through their meritocratic systems.

This has guided our mission since 2017, when we wrote our first piece of car dealer-focused software in Jerusalem. We're still at it every day since and are gratefully learning more and more from our customers and partners as we go.

In this short book, we share why we see Customer Data Platforms (CDPs) and artificial intelligence (AI) as the key to securing the future of car dealerships, and offer dealers practical advice on how to best establish a working data strategy.

We don't believe we have all the answers. Our core objective with this book is to offer a birds-eye view of the future automotive landscape and suggest key considerations for dealers as they build the dealerships of tomorrow.

We hope this book is helpful to you and look forward to continuing the conversation.

Aharon, Eliav, and Yishai
Jerusalem, Israel, January 2024

Chapter 1: The End

August 1, 2047

Andrew looked out over his lot. There were just a few Toyotas left, their curves and sleekly sloped driver bubbles glinting in the late summer shadows of the fading Minnesota light.

He let his thoughts wander back 50 years, to a bright summer day when he, then a young boy, witnessed his father's pride as the first ever Rav4 in the Midwest rolled up to Warden Toyota. He remembered the smell of the diesel burning car carrier and the rumble of the new vehicles as they were offloaded.

"But my, how times have changed," Andrew whispered to himself.

He stepped outside the dealership showroom and took a deep breath. His loyal dealership team, the 50 remaining souls of a legion that once numbered in the thousands, quietly gathered around him on the lot, forming a loose circle. The mood was somber.

Amanda, his dedicated general manager of 20 years, walked through the crowd, passing out memento pins featuring a small picture of the dealership building; something small to acknowledge this moment for this was the end of an era; the end of Warden Auto.

But this ending was bigger than just the end of Warden Auto.

Much bigger.

The shuttering of Warden's Toyota dealership also marked the closing of the last family-owned franchise dealership in North America.

Just 10 years ago, such a scenario would have seemed like science fiction. Warden Auto was at its peak – most dealers were.

During the post-pandemic decade, following the restoration of supply chains and the economic recovery, car sales hit an all-time high. It didn't hurt that Tesla's stock had crashed in the late 20s, and that traditional OEMs, realizing their distribution networks were their golden goose, had extended an olive branch to dealers. OEMs started pumping out innovative, futuristic new products, and by 2029, car dealers were thriving.

The industry took off like a rocketship. Regional dealer groups like Warden's rose from the recession years of the mid-2020s and hit the 2030s flush with cash to spend. Nearly two million employees were banking record bonuses, and the future looked bright for their families and communities.

At least, that's what it looked like on the surface.

While car dealerships reveled in their newfound success, a counterplot steadily advanced behind the scenes.

Hidden under a smokescreen of complacency fueled by the OEMs' dealer-first policy, several nextgen car companies, including Tesla, desperately seeking a way back to the top, together with some traditional OEMs, were secretly collaborating with big-box monopoly retailers like Walmart, Target and Amazon.

The mission? An all-out assault on the legislative advantages that dealers had fought to maintain since the Depression era.

Codenamed "DropShip," the coalition was backed by tens of billions of lobbying dollars. This unlikely cabal was on the verge of a historic federal ruling, one that would declare illegal the longstanding state-level protections for local dealers. To deliver the coup de grâce, the coalition also worked to advance a vicious tax regime that would undercut the ability of car dealers to compete against these global retail companies.

On June 7, 2033, a day memorialized by dealers as "Treachery Tuesday," the United States Federal Government passed the proposed legislation.

Within weeks, Walmart debuted its first megalot near Marietta, GA, loaded with 30,000 new vehicles from 10 OEMs, complete with a full trade-in lot and 50 service lanes.

Target followed soon after, taking AutoNation private in the course of just one weekend, introducing new cars into their extensive store network.

Amazon, having secretly accumulated a massive number of open lots across North America, snapped up Carmax, Asbury, Lithia, and PepBoys. They then launched their network of dealerships, offering online shopping, home delivery, and on-demand repair services.

In just a few short years, several major OEMs were acquired by the mega-retailers. These market behemoths, now vertically integrated and unencumbered by regulation and restrictive OEM covenants, used their scale, tech, and adjacent business assets to downscale employee wages, squeeze suppliers, and crush traditional dealership price margins.

As the 2030s rolled on, these newly formed monster automotive retailers backed by massive destination-style car lots began to aggressively market to their retail customer bases. Emails, ads, and tie-ins with other sales promotions ("Pick up your Christmas tree and take it home in your brand new F-150 Monsoon, now available at Target stores nationwide."), along with owned banks and insurance companies, and a broad range of services and products quickly skyrocketed their business success.

Dealers, hard-pressed to keep up with the price pressure and the marketing firepower, fell to the back of the pack, running on their limited cash with rising floor plan expenses hanging over them like the sword of Damocles.

One by one, dealers began to retreat, ceding to the new automotive overlords. By 2040, the dealership star that had shone so brightly since the early 1900s crashed to earth with a rapidity reminiscent of the Blockbuster and Netflix saga.

Mass layoffs led to ex-dealership employees moving over to work on the big box auto lots - but the pay was poor, the atmosphere was bleak, and the management implemented strict policies that made the day-to-day working experience unbearable.

Tax loopholes engineered by legions of lobbyists pulled money from the state coffers and many charities suffered as the dealerships and their owners – mainstays of local sponsorships and philanthropies – were forced to pull back on their not-for-profit giving.

By 2045, only a handful of dealerships remained, mostly in Texas and Michigan, but by the winter of 2047, the family-owned dealership was a thing of the past - except for one: Warden Toyota, the last of the car dealers.

As Warden's employees gathered around to bid farewell on this final day, the media drones began to arrive, floating at ground level and overhead to cover the historic closing ceremony of the last dealership.

Andrew, uncharacteristically overwhelmed with emotion, turned to Amanda, who was preparing to lower the flag at the over sixty-year-old store for the very last time.

"Amanda," Andrew asked, "How is it that we dealers who epitomize competition ultimately lost the race?"

Amanda paused for a moment in careful consideration, her hands holding the dancing flag's rope against the oncoming wind.

"It didn't have to be this way," she said, shaking her head.

"We had the edge. We had transformed - moved to one price, updated our facilities, and created a smooth digital flow. Public perception of car dealers had shifted to positive. We could have evolved into our own niche Amazon and held on. Our service was so much better than theirs and customers trusted us," she continued.

"I think it was the recipe for innovation that we lacked, partly because the industry failed to recognize that the good of the whole would require some sacrifice by individuals. Sharing, collaborating, and getting the data right was a must. In the end, our competition had a better customer data strategy than we did. That, coupled with their scale, was just too much for us to overcome."

With that, Amanda pulled on the rope and the last dealership team watched in somber silence as the flag slowly drifted down with the setting sun.

Chapter 2: Strategizing for Doomsday

To many, this scenario may seem far-fetched or overly alarmist, but the reality is, it's already starting to play out in the here and now. With Amazon's recent announcement of its intention to list Hyundai vehicles, big box retail is taking the baby steps it needs to make big moves.

The stakes for the US economy could not be higher when it comes to the automotive industry. Car dealerships represent a form of regulated capitalism, where legislation "by the people," in the form of Congress, has preserved some societal goods at the expense of others.

To the average non-industry person, it may look anticompetitive to legislatively force car manufacturers to sell through franchised dealerships - but there is substantial logic behind those decisions.

Extreme "laissez faire" capitalism has always created problems for a market economy. Unregulated or unchecked, businesses have a tendency to swing to extremes, leveraging scale to optimize costs for consumers beyond what's good for society. Hence, the widespread appreciation of anti-monopoly laws and wise regulation of non-competitive sectors.

Indeed, the Walmartification of the car business would reduce costs per vehicle, but consider the implications: it would lead to lower-paying jobs for the millions of families living in the automotive supply chain, the detachment of dealers from their community roots and philanthropic and business accountabilities, and the reduction of incoming taxes that go to fund education and infrastructure.

The car dealer at its best is truly a community animal. We once took a ride with David Kelleher from David Dodge in Philadelphia and, in the span of an hour in Dave's car, three separate local civic organizations called about philanthropic initiatives and events. Dave also stopped for ten minutes to chat with a local couple who had bought cars from him over the years and wanted his advice.

This energy – community oriented, local-minded, involved, and accountable – will be familiar to every dealer owner reading this book. It would all be lost in a future where major retail takes over.

We are not speaking theoretically. Similar scenarios have already and repeatedly occurred in other industries and retail markets. The "Wal-Mart Effect" is a widely discussed phenomenon whereby the opening of a superstore like Walmart can kill off the traditional small-to-medium businesses in the towns within the hundred or so mile radius of the store.

So, how is it possible for these quintessential family-owned community businesses to stay resilient when competing against the giants?

Throughout history, we have witnessed dozens of David and Goliath scenarios, where the small or "weak" have beat the strong and mighty. In these situations, the secret to success is to focus on an innovative edge or to create a unique advantage for a particular niche, rather than for a broad swath of markets.

In the automotive industry, dealers will preserve their advantage by getting the customer experience right, and specializing in supporting the complex emotional purchase of a vehicle.

However, to leverage this potential advantage, dealers will have to work together towards a different industry standard when it comes to data and innovation.

Dealers may excel in service and be amazing at guiding car sales but, if their data ecosystem isn't set up, they will never be able to stand up to the competition. Moreover, if their data isn't accessible and organized, even the best innovators will find it too difficult to build technology and solutions that can give dealers the competitive edge they need going forward.

If dealers get the formula right, combining their customer-service orientation with a real data infrastructure, strategy, and the force multiplier of AI, they can compete against the incoming industry Goliaths that are plotting to capture the industry.

The Startup Industry

The power of innovation is not lost on us as we sit here in Israel in 2024.

We founded Fullpath in Israel – a country that is often known as the "Startup Nation." While it is a small, young country of just over 9 million people that is far from major markets, Israel has still managed to drive a startup and technology ecosystem that leads the world with the third largest number of companies listed on Nasdaq, a fact that tends to come as a surprise to many.

There is no doubt that the recipe for startup success is complex, but Israel has one key component that has helped build some of the greatest technology companies in the world: a culture of creativity and innovation that permeates every facet of the country.

Israeli society encourages people to take risks and go for gold by de-stigmatizing failure and not reacting in disbelief to big or unusual ideas. The Israeli public and private sectors have, over time, worked to eliminate some of the obstacles that typically get in the way of startups, by offering facilities, funding, and other infrastructure to actively support and cultivate a culture of innovation.

We believe that the same energy that permeates our country can power the dealer-advantage in the future.

The energy of the automotive industry often reminds us of that same energy we feel in Israel. We see it as the "Startup Industry."

People in the automotive industry are restive, innovative, daring, and imaginative. Dealers, leaders, and vendors are generous with their time, and are open to taking risks in the name of innovation. This culture of generosity and sharing has inspired us at every step along the way.

Back when we first started the company, we were desperately trying to learn everything about the car business by interning at car dealerships, talking to any and every position at the dealership, and reading every relevant book we could get our hands on, with Dale Pollak's "Velocity," featuring prominently.

Aharon, having read all of Dale's books, sent a note to Dale on a lark during a flight to Chicago, asking if he'd ever have a few minutes to chat. Within a short time, Dale wrote back inviting Aharon to visit his home. Aharon spent an hour soaking up insights and feedback from Dale, learning much about the car business thanks to Dale's generosity with his time.

It is this type of openness to sharing and collaboration that is so characteristic of the automotive industry. The examples from our early days are endless, like how Debbie Waines and Mike Miller at the John Elway Dealership Group, who piloted Fullpath's early website enhancement technology, shared valuable insights with us along the way and saw the big picture through various new product hiccups. This spirit of innovation, paired with the energy of sharing and collaboration, is an asset that many industries lack.

The automotive industry is a real community. The challenge, however, lies in the fact that this spirit of innovation exists within a challenging environment when it comes to infrastructure, data, and technological collaboration.

THAT'S WHAT THIS BOOK IS ABOUT: HOW WE CAN GET THE INFRASTRUCTURE PIECE RIGHT SO THAT THE INDUSTRY'S CREATIVE ENERGY CAN BE FULLY UNLEASHED FOR THE SAKE OF THE GREATER GOOD.

Given the opportunity, and without the data obstacles that currently exist, we are confident that the smart folks of the automotive industry will drive forward tremendous innovation that will benefit this segment of the economy's future. By working together to get it done right, car dealerships can become a formidable force that can challenge even a relentless, multi-headed monster such as Amazon.

We do not know exactly what form the fight will take, but we do know that it's coming.

Dealers looking to make it out in one piece must level up - and fast - in order to beat the retail giants and other spoiler players at their own game. To do this, we must come together as an industry and start by first getting one thing right: the data.

Let's get into it.

Chapter 3: Enabling Data Weaponization

Data is a powerful weapon and global retail conglomerates have it by the truckload.

Modern data infrastructure is designed to capture nearly every data point a business generates in real time, all the time. Businesses that implement a proper data infrastructure – one that cleans the data and makes it useful to a broad swathe of users – have virtually unlimited potential in enhancing customer satisfaction and driving the kind of loyalty that improves the bottom line.

For too long, the automotive industry has settled for the status quo. Dealership data is, to be frank, an absolute mess. Dealers have resigned themselves to the fact that they must use multiple systems with inflexible software, few of which speak to each other and where data syncing, if it happens at all, is sporadic, inefficient, and often extremely manual.

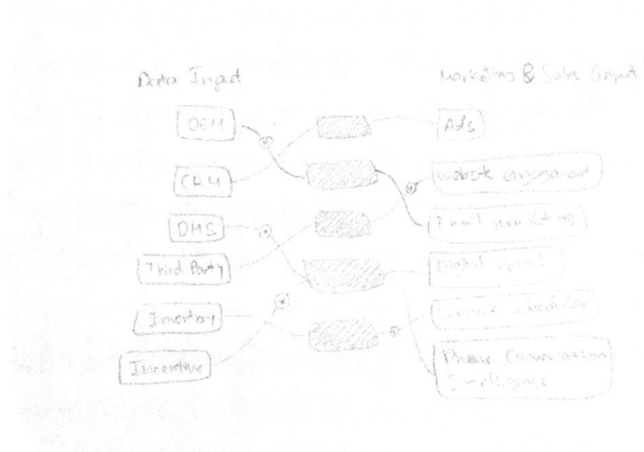

This disconnected data disaster has done nothing less than lay waste to possibilities that exist within the automotive industry.

In today's modern retail and commerce world, a data strategy is no longer a "nice-to-have." It's a must-have. Dealers looking to play the long game must get serious about developing an effective data infrastructure and strategy.

The Painful Process of Coming Up to Speed

The automotive industry must undergo a transformation that, as a mentor of ours once put it, "is good for the species, but is going to be very bad for many individual animals."

What does this mean, practically?

Creating a coherent data ecosystem is going to require a major change in behavior that will have an immediate cost, but will ultimately serve the greater good.

- Vendors will have to make capital investments that will improve their technology infrastructure;
- Vendors will have to publish low cost, robust APIs (Application Programming Interfaces);
- Vendors will have to choose to more freely share data that they currently protect in a monetized, walled-off gardens;
- Dealers will have to suspend some of the skepticism and doubt that often characterizes their software choices, and build long-term, strategic partnerships with vendors;
- Dealers will have to invest in additional team members who are skilled in the fields of data, technology, and analysis.

We don't shy away from acknowledging that bringing the industry up to speed may increase dealership expenses in the short term, and will likely reshape the current vendor landscape. It undoubtedly will.

When it comes to data, the vendor culture in parts of the industry can be compared to that of a "rentier state," a country that makes most of its money by renting out its natural resources, like oil or minerals, instead of through competitive business and innovative progress.

Dealer data, which has been aggregated into certain platforms over the years, is controlled similarly to how oil is controlled as a resource:

If anyone wants access to oil, they have to pay for it. Everyone who touches the oil along the way is going to be charged for it, especially if they want the pipeline to pass through their territory. What's really wild is that even the "owners" of the oil (ok, we went a bit too deep with this metaphor - we mean dealers) may have to pay a third party to access it.

Moreover, every data source has its unique specifications. Returning to our oil distribution analogy, if you want to pipe oil from one state to another, you need to build a pipeline with specific dimensions. If you want to then pipe it to another state, it will require you to build a completely different pipeline with its own specifications in addition to the first pipeline. In some states, the oil doesn't flow through pipes, but instead uses a railroad system, necessitating the building of an entirely different transport system to enable access.

To add to the confusion, every state has a different name for the same oil, and sometimes, those same names describe an entirely different resource in another state. Some states are closed off entirely from the oil business, while in others, the oil is entirely inaccessible to everyone but the state.

In short, making sense of the existing systems to leverage the oil in a smooth and efficient manner is next to impossible.

The chaos in this metaphor perfectly encapsulates the challenges in the automotive data ecosystem. Consider these four real world examples that illustrate the complex challenges vendors and dealers face in making sense of their data:

1. Let's say a vendor pulls data from your CRM or from one CRM in your dealer group. Included in that data is a column called 'First_Name.' In another part of the CRM or, in a CRM from a different store in your group, the column is called 'First Name.' In another, it is succinctly called 'Name.' While this may seem trivial, in your destination table (more on this later), each of these would be considered different columns. This likely sounds familiar as you have probably experienced this issue first-hand when performing imports and exports from various software systems.

2. Some industry CRMs do not track shoppers, (i.e., the aggregation of different leads into one

resolved "data entity," which we call a "shopper,") and only track leads as the core entity. Other CRMs track shoppers as the core entity and those shoppers generate leads. When you think about it in terms of taking that data and activating it to further your business goals, the CRMs that don't track shoppers end up missing out on a massive amount of critical data that can adversely affect the performance of AI and marketing automation tools, putting users at a severe disadvantage.

3. Think ahead to the future where you may want to make a switch in your CRM provider. To do so, you will need to transfer your existing data from one system to another. In your current CRM, your customer ID field is called 'Prospect ID.' Your new CRM provider calls the same field, 'Customer ID' and the 'Prospect ID' field actually refers to what your current CRM calls the 'Lead ID.' While it does not make transferring providers impossible, it does make transfering your data over to your new CRM extremely complicated, frustrating, and time consuming. This complexity often deters dealers from switching CRM providers, even if it could benefit them in the long run.

4. Now, this example might seem extreme, but we have seen it happen time after time at multiple dealerships across multiple OEMs. Consider the

fields, 'Make,' 'Model,' and 'Trim.' Within the same dealership's website, the Jeep Wrangler 4xe Sahara could be listed in 2 different ways: in one place as 'Model: Wrangler 4xe' and 'Trim: Sahara,' and in a second place on the exact same dealership website, 'Model: Wrangler' with the 'Trim' listed as 'Sahara 4xe.' This inconsistency makes reviewing analytics and understanding the performance of your vehicles and advertising incredibly challenging because your data points are scrambled across different fields.

These data challenges are everywhere in automotive. For the industry to progress, we need real change that creates standardization, frameworks for collaboration, and ultimately, full interoperability of data.

The Challenge of Change & How NADA Can Help

So, how can this change take place?

It's certainly not simple. It requires vendors and dealers to act without any immediate or obvious incentive. Sometimes, in fact, the incentive may seem like a negative as some vendors may lose revenue and dealers might experience reduced productivity and increased expenses during the transition period. However, in order to protect the future of the industry, it has to be done.

Here we look to the National Automotive Dealer Association (NADA) as a possible lever:

If NADA is to take up a new industry reform issue, it should be this: the encouragement of unified data standards across the industry, the reduction of gratuitous gatekeeper fees for data, investment in "refactoring," i.e. redesigning and recoding old out of date APIs, and a broad dissemination modern APIs.

There are folks out there in the industry advocating for these changes, including Brian Pasch with his industry-spanning work on GA4 standards and now CDPs, and David Kain with his work on standardization of data fields across a large set of 20 groups. That said, the change has to be much bigger and come much faster. For this reason, NADA is probably the best chance we have for implementing and effectuating these changes.

In our view, NADA should be seeking to influence the role that data and data-interoperability will play in the automotive industry. The change can come from benchmarks, reports, and advocacy. For example, NADA could add an annual benchmark report on vendor data interoperability, and also begin to survey and measure dealership data scope, data hygiene, and data infrastructure spend.

Along with this, NADA should open courses in its various educational programs to train dealers and expose them to best practices in data structuring, hygiene, warehousing, and API usage.

NADA leadership should also be spending time with key vendors that house major data hubs and encouraging them to build modern APIs.

Our advocacy for the centrality of data in the dealership business doesn't imply that dealers need to become software engineers, though we firmly believe that every dealership will eventually hire technical experts and data science folk. Rather, we believe that dealerships should familiarize themselves with how data infrastructure impacts their business.

NADA should also provide a place for vendors to highlight their API development, host a regular conference call to keep this subject front and center, and provide incentive grants, similar to a government, for vendors to invest in and hit certain API standards.

We believe dealers can take a huge leap in this space, as there is indeed an inbuilt affinity to technology in the automotive industry. As our friend Ben Hadley from AutoGenius has pointed out, dealers were among the first businesses to adopt new technologies. In fact, dealerships were so successful at integrating technology in the era before the modern internet and cloud that it "enabled" dealers to arrive late to the adoption of newer technologies that are now considered essential.

It is the push by NADA coupled with the aforementioned initiatives by other industry players that can put dealers back in a pioneering position instead of playing catch-up.

Nothing less than the future of the industry is at stake.

Not Your 1990s APIs

The starting point, as we've argued for years, is APIs. With the advent of a CDP-backed strategy for dealers, APIs have become even more critical than before.

It isn't enough for APIs to just exist, they need to be useful to dealers, a process that will require vendors to collaborate on a much deeper level.

To highlight the practical impact of good APIs, we'll use a CRM as an example, but you can easily replace CRM with DMS, specialized ad platform, email platform, website, or just about any other data source in play at a typical dealership. All of them need functioning APIs to fully empower dealers, vendors, innovators, and thus, the industry as a whole.

Let's look at a use case involving the CRM - specifically at how Fullpath's Customer Data Platform (CDP) leverages CRM data, among other data sources.

A robust Customer Data Platform (CDP) connects "data silos" at the dealership in real-time in order to know a lot about many of the shoppers coming to a dealership website.

Take the example of a shopper we'll call "Jill."

Jill has left a ten year long data trail at the dealership spread across numerous different "silos," including the CRM, DMS, website, email, ad platforms, and others. In most dealerships, these data silos remain isolated, meaning that the usefulness of this data trail is limited. However, when these data silos are brought together in a CDP, the data can be pulled to create a cohesive, unified, 360° shopper profile for Jill. This is where the magic happens.

When Jill visits the dealership's website, this unified 360° profile enables the dealerships to know everything important about her instantaneously, including that she is interested in a certain truck, is focused on a specific lease special, likes a particular color, has positive equity in her current vehicle, has previously mentioned in a phone call with the dealer that she is looking to buy in the next few months, and that she is ending her payments on her current vehicle in exactly two months' time.

This mountain of information can deeply impact the dealership's next move and determine whether or not Jill will go on to make a purchase from the dealership.

For this data gathering process to work well, it needs to be done persistently and programmatically, through technology and automations rather than by manual spreadsheet uploads. This is where APIs make a tremendous impact.

Consider the CRM: If the Customer Data Platform (CDP) cannot easily connect to a CRM through a quality API, it will have a much harder time pulling out information on an ongoing and reliable basis. This means that when Jill hits the website, critical information may be missing – like the fact she had an appointment scheduled – leading the information in the CDP to be less accurate and less useful.

For the benefit of the dealer, CRMs should offer low-cost APIs that provide all the information that's needed to properly connect the data source. These APIs should be affordable, reliable, and easily accessible. This is a critical step in opening the industry up to innovation, one that will allow vendors to give Jill the best possible customer experience with the dealership.

While at Fullpath, we've found ways to work around the lack of APIs in the automotive industry, having APIs would enable others to do what we have done, thereby increasing the potential for innovation (and our developers certainly won't complain about having to spend less time working around the obstacles). While advocacy around the issue of APIs is very much under discussion by industry actors, it is still viewed as optional, rather than as a requirement.

CDP Superpowers

We'll get down to the specifics of CDPs later on but first, let's spend some time on the outcomes of partnering CDPs with APIs. Take a moment and imagine the APIs exist, or that you are using a CDP partner like Fullpath that has leveraged existing APIs and built workarounds for instances where APIs don't exist.

Instead of asking, "How do I connect my data?" you might find yourself thinking, "Now that my data is connected and I have invested in a CDP, what is a CDP really good for in my day-to-day process? How will it help me sell more cars?"

Consider this scenario of vendor collaboration between systems, as orchestrated by a CDP:

Jill, our shopper, clicks on a paid ad featuring a specific lease offer on a particular vehicle. Let's imagine it's an offer on a Ford F-150, just to make it easier to follow.

The CDP now knows Jill's vehicle of interest is an F-150 because of how the advertising and website are tagged. The CDP also knows the details of what may have caught her attention in the first place: the specific lease offer, the car color, and others.

The CDP then takes this data and informs the Fullpath website-integrated chatbot that Jill is excited about the specific lease offer or the specific vehicle in a specific color. The CDP also sends over a list of recommended vehicles to recommend to Jill. The chatbot receives this information and, while chatting with Jill, prioritizes that lease offer and other vehicle options with similar characteristics to the car she has already shown interest in.

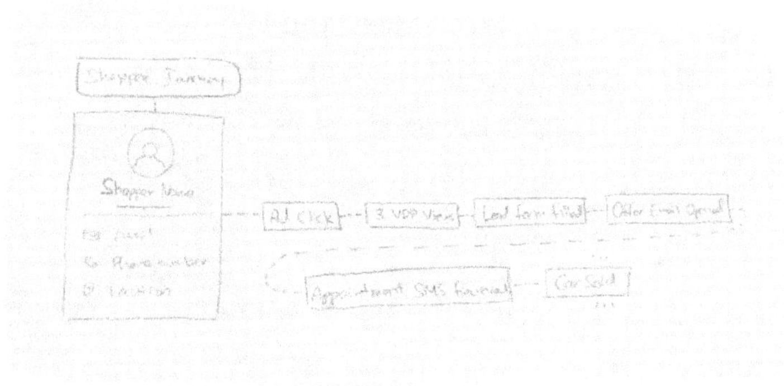

The chatbot will also put up a small persistent tab banner featuring the lease offer she initially showed interest in. This will make it easy for Jill to find the original offer and save her the hassle of having to scour the website to find it later after she navigates around the site. This creates a multifaceted positive shopping experience that is bolstered by the chat which can engage her directly with information and details about things we already know she is interested in.

This example demonstrates the true benefit of a connected data ecosystem and it is something that already works great *within* the Fullpath software universe.

"Aha!" you say. "What if the dealer is using a different chat on their website, like those offered by CarNow, Gubagoo, or ActiveEngage, instead of the Fullpath chat?"

Not a problem - in theory, at least.

In an ideal world, the Fullpath CDP would be able to send the same information via our API to a non-Fullpath chat provider. That chat provider would then be able to use the information to make their chat tool more useful for Jill. These chat products would then feed information back into our CDP to make it smarter ahead of Jill's next encounter with the dealership.

This is entirely possible with today's technologies, and it's something we'd love to see happen in a less fictional sense. However, it would require all vendors - and dealers - to actively collaborate and, in some cases, lose out on some business (in the scenario above, Fullpath would be losing the case to use our chat specifically, since there would be a seamless connection to other industry chats that could communicate with the core CDP). We believe this sacrifice is absolutely worthwhile if it means taking the industry to the next level.

Completing the Circle

To better understand the power of connected data, let's move beyond the dealer's first-party ecosystem.

Say Jill, our steadfast shopper, leaves the dealership website – a common occurrence with high-funnel shoppers – and visits a car listing site. In an ideal world, Fullpath's CDP could send Jill's behavior over to the car listing site using an API when she visits the dealer's VDP on the third party website. This data would include the specific offer she clicked on that initially brought her to the dealership website, along with any relevant insights and instructions based on CRM or DMS data. That data could then naturally flow into Jill's extended shopping experience on and off the dealership's website, with the third-party website sending data back via API to the CDP, further enhancing the customer experience back on the dealer side when Jill returns.

But Jill's customer experience wouldn't end there.

As a next step, the CDP could provide rich data to the dealership's outreach platform, like Fullpath's "Audience Activation" platform, that sends data-backed lead-nurture emails and SMS campaigns to shoppers and customers. This data-driven marketing would not be limited to Fullpath, of course. With proper interoperable APIs, platforms would be able talk to one another and dealers using technology from friends of ours like Foureyes or Outsell, would also be able to obtain the CDP data via API. With this data in hand, the outreach platform could then send a morning email to Jill to inform her about a great opportunity she may have missed in her browsing, both on and off the site.

Alongside this, the CDP could send information to a sales tool, similar to Fullpath's soon-to-be-released "Sales Enablement" product. The sales tool would then trigger an email or notification to the salesperson at the dealership that includes a log of Jill's activity, along with a suggested personalized offer or deal that they can leverage in their timely follow-up phone call.

Why is this connected experience possible for Jill, across vendors, websites, and platforms (at least in theory)?

It all comes down to CDPs and APIs that connect all sorts of data including equity data and lenders, website behavior, CRM history, DMS service records, and more. This comprehensive integration ultimately allows the salespeople and marketing platforms to tailor specific deals and offers that match this shopper's equity position and buying profile, providing the shopper with just the right amount of personalization at the right time to seal a deal.

Have we made our point yet?

A new data regime in the automotive industry is absolutely critical to progress and, in our opinion, APIs are the key building block that can enable dealers to fight back against forces that seek to undermine the industry as it stands today. CDPs play a critical role in bringing this to fruition.

As you can now see, to truly activate the dealer-data advantage and compete with what the future might bring, it will take a complete reshaping of the dealership and vendor landscape when it comes to data interoperability and APIs.

This change would be for the industry's collective benefit and the dealership industry as a whole has to make it a priority. But before that can happen, we need to understand what a dealer-data strategy really looks like and that requires a trip down into the details, deep into the weeds, where wisdom begins.

Chapter 4: Into the Weeds

Practically speaking, there are three phases to creating an effective data strategy: mapping and extracting; visualizing and analyzing; and automating marketing and enabling sales efforts. Let's take a quick dive into each of these phases.

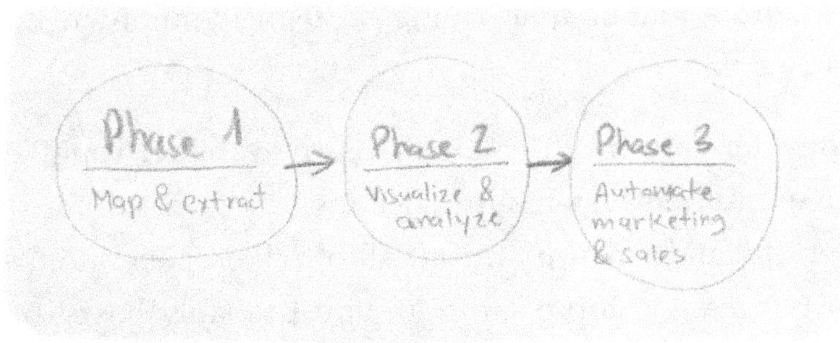

Phase 1: Mapping & Extracting

To truly understand the complexities at play, it is important to understand the difference between first and third-party data:

First-party data is data that you own. When a shopper fills out a form on your website and provides you with their contact information, that is first-party data. It is "first," in the sense that the person provided the data to you directly and you did not receive it through a middleman.

By contrast, third-party data is data that another party owns that they then use to help drive traffic, leads, and ideally, sales to your dealership. For example, when you pay Facebook to run ads on their platform, they may be using their own data to target shoppers. This data is third-party data because you do not own that data, Facebook does. When you pay Facebook to advertise using their audiences, you are paying them to use their first-party data (aka, third-party data to you) to build ad audiences, rather than doing so using your own first-party data.

Consider your own dealership as an example. You likely have multiple systems in place including a DMS, CRM, website, and email platform, all of which generate first-party data. On top of all that, you probably have some other external vendors in place as well, such as a data vendor, an advertising agency, a car listing website like

Cars.com, or something else, which may provide you with third-party data.

Now that we understand that distinction, let's get down to the practical stuff.

Think about dealership data as a sort of supply chain. You have multiple manufacturers that are each producing their own data in silos and you need to find a way to bring them all together into one place to get to the bottom line.

Phase 1 is about understanding which data sources are in play at your dealership, so that you can get them all flowing into one place.

The More First-Party Data, the Better.

You've probably heard the old saying "less is more," but when it comes to data collection, the more you have, the better off you are. With a cookieless reality looming in the not-so-far-off future, it's imperative for dealerships to own as much first-party data as they can.

You can no longer bank on Facebook and Google to target your audiences; you're going to need your own clean, usable data, if you're going to successfully market and sell to your customers.

Modern data extraction and organization into a usable system happens through a process called ETL - Extract, Transform, and Load. ETL processes may have been called by different names over time, but they are as old as databases themselves, stretching back to IBM in the 1960s.

A more modern way to think of this process is by comparing it to streaming. Data is streamed from all your important data silos into one framework, often known as a data lake or data warehouse (there are differences, but the specifics are not important here), where it is cleaned up, sorted, and organized for use.

To get started with the data mapping process, take a look at these data sources:

1. **DMS and CRM** - These are your most critical sources of first-party data. They hold millions of customer and inventory data points that offer a lot of opportunity. Now, neither acts as a single source of truth which is why streaming the data into a centralized platform so it can be cross-referenced is the best way to go. Keep in mind, your DMS is only going to show data on sold or serviced. Your CRM leads, going back years, can be a valuable source to expand your first-party data targeting set.

2. **Website** - Your website generates a wealth of first-party information, including shopper behavioral data that can be used to build shopper profiles for marketing and sales activities - but more on that later. Here, the key

is to connect behavior on the website to real shoppers.

3. **Advertising** - Your existing advertising data sources, such as Google, Facebook, and others, offer you a tremendous amount of data on ad performance, ROI, engagements, clicks, etc. All of this data can be pulled in to help create a more complete profile of your shoppers and develop a clearer picture of what has worked and what hasn't in your marketing efforts. Specifically, when done right, you can use the ad-click data from a specific shopper to know more about what they need or want.

4. **Third-party data sources on your domain** - This includes plugins on your website that theoretically should be "first-party" conversion points. These sources often operate in iFrames, which are essentially mini websites that are piped into your website. For all intents and purposes, unless specified otherwise, they control the data, leaving you at the mercy of the vendor and the data they are willing to share.

5. **Third-party sources** - This includes external advertising websites like Cars.com or AutoTrader and may also include data vendors like Experian, and others. Your VINs on the endemic sites attract behavior and leads - if you gain access to this data, it can help create enriched shopper profiles. That said, this data is

harder to gain access to and will likely require a powerful technology partner to secure.

Once you have your dealership data sources mapped out, you can begin extracting your data and start streaming into one place. That's when the cleaning process can begin.

While, in an ideal world, you could easily do this on your own, realistically, it is best to work with a partner. You can choose to build your own data warehouse, or you can work with companies that offer this solution turnkey, as part of their CDP offering.

Unified Data ≠ Clean Data

Why is clean data so critical? Let's take a look at a practical example that builds on an example we discussed earlier:

Let's say you pull out data from your CRM. With just a little bit of digging, you will find that many records have duplicates and near-duplicates.

What is a near-duplicate, you ask?

It is a case where it is obvious that the record reflects the same "person" or "shopper" as another record but, due to a typo, a single different data point (like, for example, a home phone number versus a mobile phone number), or a particular CRM setting, it is marked as an entirely separate record.

In our research we found that often, 30% of CRM entries are duplicate or near-duplicate records and, in some cases, that number can go as high as 50%.

When you add in the DMS, third-party forms, and other sources, numerous instances of the same shopper will appear. Combined with the column name mess we described earlier ("First_Name," "Name") and other data gaps, the resulting "unified" dataset is really just chaos all dressed up to look nice. So, while it's great that you can export and compile your data into a single destination table, your table is incapable of identifying duplicate or near-duplicate information.

In the automotive industry this sort of data confusion exists everywhere. There are at least two CRMs in the industry that we have personally encountered where the same data is named differently within their own backend. In one case, this is because two systems were merged into one CRM. In another case, there is no real explanation for it and most likely reflects different archaeological layers of when and how the system was built over the last 15+ years.

In numerous cases the challenge is slightly different. The CRM may incorporate data from the DMS where data like "First Name" may be listed with slight variations - ALL CAPS, for example, versus CRM inputs which are in regular case usage.

It's endless, really, but don't despair - it is all resolvable, and solvable.

Once your data has been brought together into one centralized location, the next step is to clean it. In the data industry, this is called performing "data hygiene."

Many in the automotive industry believe there is a data hygiene silver bullet that can be used to solve everything, say, a third-party vendor that can process and clean lists. The truth is - at least in our experience - that there is no silver bullet for building a truly clean data layer; all data layers will have some impurities.

At Fullpath, we see hygiene as a process that starts with analysis and cleaning rules; some more complex and algorithmic, and others built on basic common sense, like resolving fields that refer to the same thing with different names, eliminating duplicate information, creating unified shopper profiles, fixing truncated email addresses due to CRM or DMS field lengths, and solving more complex issues like near-duplicates, by looking at which phone number or email, for example, is most active in the dealership data.

Sometimes, third-party vendors do come in handy, especially when it comes to enriching shopper profiles with opt-in data that dealers don't own. At Fullpath, we are always cautious with third party vendors as we have high-standards when it comes to data privacy and ethics, something dealers are embracing as regulations

powering "new school" solutions like marketing automation, is the name of the game going forward.

To envision the possibilities, we spend a lot of time with industry strategists who have helped us see how dealers can further push the envelope.

Over at the Walser Automotive Group, one of our major research hubs, Mike Price has shown us how day supply and base velocity metrics matter, and we are looking at how we can overlay these outside inputs onto dealership data and offer dealers further insights.

Over the years, Walser's Colton Ray and his team of market managers, led by Kyle, Grant, and Sam, have shown us how they use complex combinations of turn reports and market share reports for both new and used vehicles to evaluate marketing impact. Jake Ehrlichman has helped us go deep on leveraging behavioral insights to understand incentives.

Partners at other groups, including Tom Drislane at Colonial Auto Group and Colin Carrasquillo at Nielsen Auto Group, have helped us understand how to lay out the data and push forward more data-formats for the various engagement arms we can deploy.

The Fullpath team is already conducting experiments on how to leverage the advertising of a dealership's competitor to create insights and reports. This will help us understand how traffic in a region is "primed," thereby influencing buyer interests through both organic and paid advertising. With this intelligence on hand, smarter decisions can be made about where to invest paid marketing dollars and how to orient inventory decisions.

The possibilities are truly endless. By analyzing and filtering your collected and cleaned data, you can provide your team with actionable information that will improve operations and increase dealership profitability.

Let's explore those possibilities in Phase Three.

Phase 3: Automating Marketing and Sales Efforts

Once your data is unified, you can begin activating it to achieve your sales and marketing departments' business goals.

When it comes to data activation and automation, marketing is usually first to benefit. AI-powered marketing platforms can help your dealership's marketing department leverage your now-unified and cleaned data to create personalized marketing campaigns at scale. This means there is no need to "spray and pray" anymore - your messaging will hit the right person at the right time, every time, because with data activation, you can create one-to-one marketing messages that fit every shopper in your CRM.

Remember the lists you handed over to your used car manager? Well, it's similar to that - only, instead of shifting your inventory goals based on website traffic, you can automatically create audiences for your marketing campaigns based on super-specific criteria.

You may, for example, want to build a list of shoppers who visited specific VDPs over the last three weeks, who have not recently submitted a lead or bought a car, and have a specific equity tranche in their vehicle. You can then leverage that list to build personalized email offers, create audiences for your social and search ads, and even launch audience extension campaigns to target potential in-market shoppers with similar characteristics.

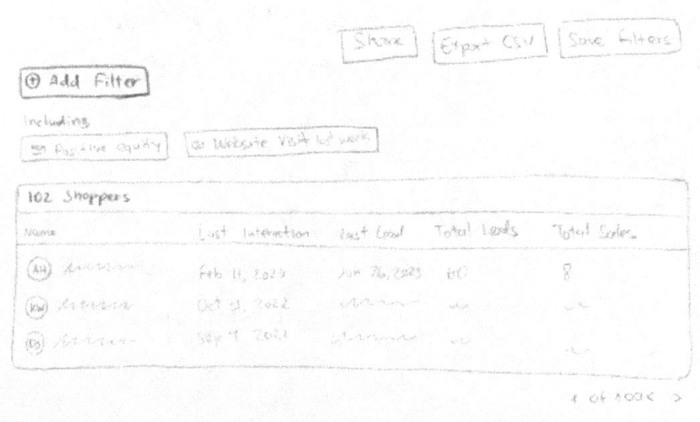

If you structure your lists correctly, you can also suppress groups from ad campaigns, for example, customers who very recently purchased a car, to keep them from receiving your latest marketing messages, saving money and reducing noise for a happy customer. This process, of course, should be totally automated by your software solutions and should not depend on busy team members.

When it comes to your used car manager, you may want to make sure that any price change they make on a vehicle – say, based on an insight in vAuto – is promptly and widely communicated across all your marketing channels. This can be done automatically once you have a clean and organized dataset and a CDP that is tied into your marketing arm.

Your unified data similarly empower your sales team. Once your data is unified and cleaned, you can layer it with AI to automatically identify non-lead in-market shoppers, based on their website browsing and email or advertising engagement. This list of potential customers can be sent to your BDS manager in the form of a daily digest, so your sales team can reach out with a little personal encouragement to nudge prospective buyers towards a purchase.

Moreover, with your unified shopper profiles, you can automatically match every individual customer to a vehicle in your inventory based on their previous interactions with your dealership and their expressed interests and needs, creating an easy sell for your sales team. You could even generate relevant financing terms based on their current equity status and preferred monthly payment. All of this can be done automatically by layering your unique, clean data set with the right technology.

Overall, your data is a critical piece in empowering your entire team. With unified, clean, activated data, you can take your sales and marketing activities to a whole new level, and build a more resilient business.

Remember, the key component here is that all of this should be automated. Today, you can do this with holistic ecosystems like Fullpath and others; in the future, these systems will hopefully be interoperable and ubiquitous.

Chapter 5: Not All Heroes Wear Capes

It is time to finally - and properly - introduce you to the real hero of our story: the Customer Data Platform (CDP). We've covered CDPs at length as part of other discussions, but they deserve their own ink because of the critical role they play.

Now, for a touch of background:

CDPs are not new, but they are new to the automotive industry. The technology has been around for over a decade, with the first mention of a Customer Data Platform appearing, to the best of our knowledge, in 2013, but the first automotive-centric CDP only hit the market in 2022.

The Fullpath CDP came together when a bunch of our team members were sitting together in our Jerusalem offices. We had all just read "Play Bigger: How Pirates, Dreamers, and Innovators Create and Dominate Markets," by Al Ramadan, Dave Peterson, Christopher Lochhead, and Kevin Maney, and were discussing how to create a category that would fit our customer data ETL and marketing automation technology .

We were looking at similar platforms outside of the automotive industry and Mike Colacchio, today, Fullpath's Chief Revenue Officer (CRO), said, "Hey, let's just bring the CDP concept to automotive - after all, it is what we do."

This idea really spoke to us. Many of the most innovative thinkers in automotive - like our friend Andrew Gordon the founder of Dealer Science - were talking about how data was coming up as a key topic in discussion with progressive dealers. He believed it was going to become mainstream and we were experiencing the same phenomenon.

From there it all happened naturally. Our VP of Marketing, Ilana Shabtay, and her team brilliantly dubbed our technology a "CDXP," wherein "X" is for experience, making us a *Customer Data and Experience Platform*. Within just a few weeks, the term "CDP" reached high prominence in the industry.

While it has taken some time for the industry to catch up, dealers have started to embrace the technology for what is: a data weaponization software that can improve operations, bolster customer relationships, and ultimately, create financially sustainable, and economically resilient dealerships that can weather any storm.

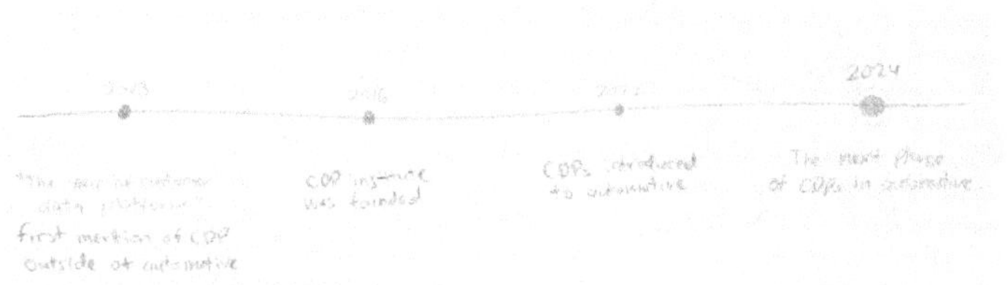

In fact, everything we described in this book thus far can be powered by a legitimate CDP. While it may sound like a big promise, we guarantee that a real CDP can deliver.

How, you ask? It's simple.

There are four key components to a real CDP that can help propel your dealership forward: data infrastructure, identity resolution, 360° shopper profiles, and API connectivity.

Let's take a closer look:

Data Infrastructure

Building your dealership's data infrastructure is the most basic part of beginning to leverage your data. CDPs are data intensive platforms that create that infrastructure for you by bringing all of the data sources already in play at your dealership into one place.

A real CDP ingests your website data, including all website shopper activity and relevant insights (i.e. the shopper spent time looking at certain features on the website), your CRM data, inventory data, DMS data, OEM offers, dealership specials, Google ads, Facebook ads, call tracking conversations and more - especially if the CDP works with a proper API.

After collecting all of this raw data, the CDP then processes it and builds a comprehensive database of every interaction your dealership has had with potential shoppers and existing customers across their shopper journey and their relationship with your business.

Once your data is fully integrated into the CDP and has gone through the cleaning and normalization process (see Component 2, Identity Resolution) you can then use the CDP's filtering and list building infrastructure. These tools allow you to slice and dice your data and gain deep insights into your shoppers' behavior and dealership operations.

Consider this very real world example, a version of which we envisioned in real time in a discussion with Ryan Pesin at Ardmore Toyota: you have to sell another

10 sedans by the end of the month in order to reach your sales quota. With a proper data infrastructure in place, you can cross-reference your data to build a list of your dealership's hottest leads. You can query your data, asking questions like, "Who in my CRM left a lead on a sedan in the last year, never made a purchase, but is now browsing my website?" You can also check if you have any former customers whose lease is coming up for renewal or whose financing terms are coming to an end in the next three months.

Your CDP, or the BI platform that your CDP feeds into, will then filter your data down to provide you with a list of golden opportunities to get those sedans sold fast, all in about 10 seconds.

In short, unifying your data within a CDP to create a proper data infrastructure makes your data more accessible so you can benefit big and reach your goals.

Identity Resolution

As we've discussed, identity resolution in the automotive space is pretty complex. You likely have multiple records for most of your shoppers. They may have submitted a lead on one page using their primary email address and then, a few weeks later, submitted a new lead using another email address - or, even more simply, they included a typo in their email, which triggered a new entry in your CRM. There are at least a dozen reasons as to why you may have multiple entries that point to one person - the real issue is how you resolve these entries into one profile and, in some cases, map that profile to a greater household made up of multiple shoppers.

A few years back, as part of a larger project, we analyzed the CRM of a dealership in the midwest with over 178,000 records of car and service leads and customers. No automotive CRM manager would be surprised to hear that nearly 30,000 of those records were duplicates. This was a major impetus for us to build algorithms, protocols, and systems to map, identify, and resolve identities.

When it comes down to it, identity resolution is essentially the process of identifying and unifying multiple entries for the same shopper that are pulled from multiple platforms - your DMS, your CRM, your website and ad data - in order to create a single, complete picture of each shopper.

Resolving these identities, and associating them with their behavior on the website and in advertising, is a real advantage to a dealership's data strategy. We had endless discussions about this topic with our friend Ashley Cavazos who, at the time, was at Walser, and is now at Demontrond Auto Group. These talks led us to study the nuances in the CRM that we could bring forward for dealer data queries. They are endless and the possibilities they present are exciting.

Identity resolution can help make your marketing more efficient by ensuring you are marketing to one person instead of four profiles that belong to the same person, saving you time, money and frustration. At the same time, it helps you create a more positive customer experience because A, the customer is not being bombarded by multiple irrelevant email or ad campaigns at every turn and B, you are working with the most updated, relevant data which means that you can target them with offers and information that actually matters to them now.

Compiled 360° Shopper Profiles

CDPs work to create 360° shopper profiles that you can leverage to personalize your approach at every touchpoint on the customer journey, based on the shopper's needs and interests. Stitching together fragmented customer data to create a cohesive and accurate customer profile from various data channels is a critical and core CDP functionality.

Putting together a complete picture of the shopper has been our obsession from day one, when we debuted our first automotive software iteration. The technology was known as "Connect" and then "Falcon." This exact challenge was the central focus of a brainstorming session we had in our early days at Jay Honda in Cleveland, our first clients, with owner, Nathan, and the marketing director, Kevin. At the time pulling everything into one picture seemed so far away. Indeed, it took years, but today we are seeing that progress come to life.

When done right, CDP-generated 360° shopper profiles should allow you to track every customer engagement with your dealership in one orderly, consolidated place. This includes any website visits, ad engagements, email engagements, dealership visits, phone calls, upcoming and past service appointments, and more so you can fully understand their shopper journey and what action should come next.

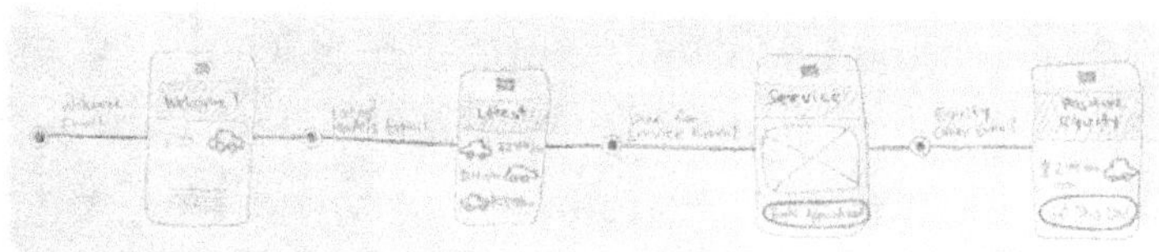

This level of data "coverage" is not possible through just the CRM or DMS. They don't reflect the full picture on their own, hence the need for a CDP or a CDP that can push data into the CRM.

API Connectivity

Yes, we're back to APIs.

While we've already spent so much ink on this subject, we are going to put down a few more pages about it, because it is so very important. Thank you for your patience, dear reader!

Application Programming Interfaces (APIs) are key to unlocking the power of the automotive industry's data which, as we previously discussed, is a *sine qua non* to competing with your powerful competitors over tomorrow's automotive landscape.

APIs allow for seamless data exchange and integration with other systems. Take, for example, Google Maps:

Businesses can pay to use Google's map API in order to integrate Google Maps on their website, making it easier for them to show customers where they are located. This exchange of data happens seamlessly with the power of an API.

In a perfect world, your siloed dealership data sources would offer a public API that is affordable and modern in architecture, to allow the different platforms to communicate with one another. This would instantly give you more control over your data, enabling you to gather data about customer preferences and behavior which can then be used to create the kind of shopping experiences that drive customer loyalty and extend customer lifecycles.

Unfortunately, this is not so common in the automotive industry.

For a CDP, a public API is critical. It allows dealers to link in other vendors and harness more of their existing data. Your data is yours and yours alone - a CDP with a public API means you can leverage your connected data by sending it out to other platforms to improve and optimize your activities.

Take a shopper who recently visited your website and looked at a specific VDP. That shopper abandoned your website, only to return a few days later - but this time, they are browsing an entirely different vehicle. Your CDP should be able to quickly identify this shift in vehicle of interest, update the data record, and send that information and related content (suggested cars, even outreach text - depending on how turnkey your CDP is, etc.) out via API to your marketing platforms - be it your AI-powered emailing system or your Google ads platform, so the shopper can automatically receive ads and emails that reflect their most recent needs and interests.

The first time we saw our CDP-backed email platform, then called Nurture, now called Audience Activation, we were blown away. Ido, our product director, who started off at the company as a developer and has been deeply involved in the development of our technology, demoed the product for us, and it was like watching magic happen before our eyes. Thousands of targeted, intelligent, totally personalized and relevant emails were instantly created by onboarding 10 years of dealer data into the system. This type of power is next-level, giving shoppers a great experience and surfacing opportunities within your data that are just waiting to be seized.

A CDP with an API (or, lacking an API, a solid ecosystem of marketing automation around the CDP), offers a strategic advantage. It allows for tactical activation of your data - and tactical data leverage is how you win.

Your CDP's API plays a critical role in the successful tactical activation of your data. Without it, your shopper would continue seeing irrelevant ads until someone manually reconfigures your audiences. This not only costs you in marketing dollars, but also harms your customer experience, which will cost you far more in the long run.

Sticking with the API theme, here is a break in your regularly scheduled programming to make another plea for API standardization in the automotive industry.

The biggest dealership threat and source of competition comes from outside players seeking to disrupt the traditional ways of the industry with technological and operational prowess. That means your vendors need to collaborate and work together to ensure dealerships are the best-run businesses in the country.

One way in which we can speed up technological progress among dealers is to standardize APIs. Currently, there are minimal standardized APIs with CRMs or any other critical dealer infrastructure that allow front-of-house vendors to seamlessly integrate. While the ADF-XML format was excellent for the industry's early evolution, that format does not allow for the type of modern read/write access and granular level detail that is required for top-of-the-line marketing automation.

Outside of the automotive industry, multi-billion dollar companies such as Salesforce and Hubspot have open and standardized APIs that allow other companies to leverage their systems to increase value for their customers. Yes, these major competitors allow for integration because they recognize that their core business and, most importantly, their customers, only benefit from the two working together.

The current process in the automotive industry is painfully slow. If we all grow the pie together, the dealership ecosystem will not just survive, but thrive. However, if we, as vendors, continue to make it difficult for each other to scale, we're not only hurting the dealers and ourselves, we're also giving full reign to what could be the most unfortunate downfall of the iconic American dealership.

*Okay, we're done (for now). Let's get back to our regularly scheduled programming.**

Without these four basic elements - data infrastructure, identity resolution, 360° shopper profiles, and APIs - a data platform cannot be considered a true CDP. You will see a lot of companies out there representing themselves as a CDP, but in reality, they are missing some core functionalities that could end up doing more harm than good for your dealership.

The Rise of the "CDP Up"

Ideally, the CDP is the brain that sits at the center of all dealership operations. When coupled with AI, it can even, in some ways, operate the dealership, or at least serve as a first officer for the general manager and as a co-pilot for many of the different functions at the dealership.

The connected data that the CDP creates allows for everything in the dealership to work in tandem. This will give the dealer – and most importantly – the shopper, a better all around experience. However, it goes beyond vendor collaboration.

Yes, chats, emails and ads will become more relevant and automated. Yes, sales people will know what to talk about with customers to make conversations more effective. Yes, every shopper interaction – whether they reach out by phone, engage digitally, or stop in at the store – will be smoother and more customer-friendly. But, the really cool thing only a CDP can offer is the ability for dealers to create a whole new lead source and, in effect, perform a sort of alchemy, where they turn data gathered over decades into sales on demand.

Indeed, the data connectivity made possible by the CDP gives dealers the ability to create sales out of data – real, true "sales generation," that could never have been achieved before.

At Fullpath, we call these, "CDP Ups."

One of our most veteran customers and a generally savvy operator, Stephen Gabbara at Szott Ford in Detroit, very succinctly described his experience with the concept of a "CDP Up:"

A few years ago, on the last day of a sales month, Stephen had an epiphany - maybe more of a quasi-fantasy, as it was an idea that felt unrealistic at the time.

He thought about how when he wakes up every morning, he uses his phone to answer a series of questions:

- What's the temperature outside?
- Will it snow today?
- How much snow is on the ground right now?
- How long will my commute to work take today?

His phone, drawing on a myriad of data sources, knows how to answer each of these questions; quickly, concisely, and for the most part, correctly.

What if his phone could do the same thing for his business? What if he could simply ask, "Which of my shoppers is up to buy a car today?"

Stephen didn't know it, but at the time, we were working on this exact concept.

On a trip to Israel to visit with our product team, Stephen shared this fantasy with Elik, one of our sharp product managers at our Tel Aviv office. Just a few months later, Elik called Stephen and said, "Hey Stephen, remember your dream of asking your phone who to call in order to sell a car today? Well, I am going to send a list to your email right now. These are five people who are <u>not</u> leads, some of whom you haven't spoken to in years, but who are about to buy a car. I'm also going to tell you which car they want, and what financing deal will best fit them. Have your team call them today."

Stephen was skeptical at first, but he was game to try. Worst case, he made a call. Best case, he made a sale.

He sent the list to one of his sales reps and asked them to make the calls. Sure enough, three of the shoppers on the lists were bullseyes.

Stephen realized he had a new concept to integrate - not a traditional phone up, store up, or internet up, but a data up or – as we now call it - a "CDP Up."

To be clear, this new up-source was actually an "up," and not a blind shot in the dark.

Sales teams are rarely motivated to churn through a 60 - 100 name list of shoppers pulled at random or by a "last touch" date extracted from a CRM or excel spreadsheet. The chances of any of those calls turning into a sale are low. "CDP Ups" on the other hand, were showing Szott Ford's salespeople, clear as day - or - clear as a showroom up, that they wanted to buy a car, and soon.

To properly service these "CDP Ups," Stephen's dealership team developed a totally different engagement technique. They don't call to pitch - in fact, they are not allowed to even mention sales-related content in the first phone call. They simply give a courtesy call to check in and say hello. This approach, respectful and reasoned, leads to a wonderful conversation that often transitions into a sales opportunity.

The reality is, most dealers don't have a handle on their first-party data, much less a working data strategy. Dealers are sitting on ten - sometimes twenty years worth of data - which should make it possible for them to be far more proactive in triangulating shoppers. It should be possible to pull from all of that data to build an opportunity list for each sales person - or for each marketing automation action - of the top people who are most likely to buy a car today.

It is very clear to us here at Fullpath that the value and potential of CDPs for driving dealership success is endless. With a touch of imagination and a heap of powerful innovation, dealerships can gain full control of their data and start leveraging it to its fullest extent, transforming into data-driven powerhouses that can overcome any attempted takedowns by future monopoly players.

Chapter 6: It's What You Do With It That Counts

TACTICAL DATA ACTIVATION

Data without activation is like trying to play Monopoly without any of the play money. Sure, you could throw the dice and move around the board, but what are you really doing?

The same goes for this experience:

You are browsing on Amazon, or another retail giant's website, looking for a new kitchen gadget or a toy for your kid. You click through a couple of options and add something to your cart. You then get distracted by an email alert or a phone call and close out the window. Within 20 minutes, an email lands in your inbox:

"Hey (insert your name here), we see you forgot to complete your checkout process. Click here to dive back in and complete your purchase. Oh, also, we found these products that you might be interested in based on your previous browsing history. You might also want to add those to your cart by simply clicking on this button."

This is something big box retailers have perfected: tactical data activation, or the art of seamless, personalized, timely engagements designed to pull you back in. The entire process happens instantly, behind the scenes, at scale, and with zero human intervention required.

It may sound intimidating and unbeatable, but here's the thing - these capabilities are not exclusive to big box retailers. Creating these holistic shopping experiences for your customers is something that is totally achievable for your dealership. All you need is (you guessed it!) a proper data infrastructure and a little AI activation magic.

Let's Talk AI

The time has come to talk about AI – just for a bit.

Artificial Intelligence (AI) has been around since the 1950s but it only more recently reached the level of dinner table talk. In the last decade or so, AI has brought us into a new era, one defined by personalization, speed and efficiency. These technologies are, of course, amazing and will lead to many useful innovations that will enable dealers to compete against big behemoths with ease.

But here's the thing: AI is only as good as the data it is trained on, which makes your CDP even more critical in taking your activities to the next level.

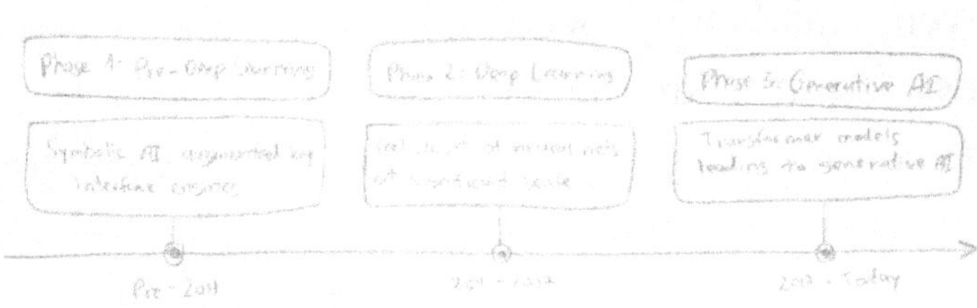

When you bring the data infrastructure of a CDP together with the activation capabilities of AI, you get so much more than just another set of automotive acronyms - you get the two core pillars you need to keep your dealership relevant and engaged as the world moves forward through the digital age.

It is the synergistic connection between a CDP and AI that helped create that seamless customer experience Amazon offered in our example. When you integrate a CDP at your dealership and combine it with AI-driven

3. **Adjusting campaigns automatically based on data insights:** AI and CDPs can help your dealership instantly respond to market trends and get your name out there on the hottest items. For example, if the AI system detects a surge in interest for a particular model in your region in the CDP data, it will automatically generate and execute more targeted ad campaigns to reach shoppers who are interested in those vehicles.

4. **Improving performance through a feedback loop:** AI and CDPs work together, constantly feeding data back and forth. This means that the AI will feed ad campaign performance data back into the CDP, so the CDP can then help the AI build more refined audiences and predict which marketing messages and formats will be most likely to engage specific shopper groups.

The possibilities are endless, really.

Remember our earlier discussion about public APIs? Well, this is one of those places where it can make or break you. When your AI and CDP are connected, your AI software will recognize any significant action taken by a shopper or customer in a marketing campaign and feed that data back into your CDP so that it becomes part of the shopper profile data for you to leverage in your next engagement. The process works both ways. If a shopper makes a move on your website or at your dealership, your CDP will feed that information back to the AI so it can make adjustments in its targeting strategy, in real-time.

The powerful synergy between AI and CDPs when it comes to data activation is really unmatched by any other solution out there. CDPs keep your data clean, maintained, and updated in real-time, in order to power your AI-driven activities. This allows you to quietly and automatically work to nurture customer satisfaction and loyalty for your dealership, without any manual effort needed on your part.

The Role of GPT AIs

When we look to the future, generative AI models – particularly those based on deep learning neural networks like GPT (Generative Pre-trained Transformer) – are leading the way. The core mechanism of these models is essentially a complex algorithmic process of character prediction, which allows them to create text that makes sense, based on the information or prompt they're given.

These models work off a specialized form of database known as a vector database. These databases encode data into vectors to help the model understand and find the right information quickly, so it can instantaneously respond to prompts. Combining the power of AI with the vectorized data is a critical part of fine-tuning the responses and generating insightful analytical predictions.

Using these AI models correctly is tricky and requires a nuanced balance. On the one hand, we need to carefully manage the vector database's exposure to the AI to make sure data security is upheld and that sensitive information is not compromised. On the other hand, we have to balance controlling how the AI model behaves to minimize mistakes while offering it the latitude it needs to generate, which is what gives it those "magical" capabilities.

This balance is important, whether the AI is being used in public-facing systems like in a dealership's chatbot, or behind the scenes in a company's internal-facing tools like we use here at Fullpath. The AI's information needs to be reliable in order for it to properly perform its core functions, yet the rules need to not be so rigid that they crush the AI's capabilities.

As generative AI continues to grow and evolve and its usage becomes more widespread, technical strategists in the dealership data ecosystem are investing a lot of effort into learning how to better understand and leverage these advanced AI capabilities. The ultimate goal is to harness these technologies to help scale dealership operations, improve customer experiences, and build future-forward, data-driven businesses.

The Cyborg Dealership: Meet Your AI Agent

When will you hire your first AI employee? We think it will be much sooner than you realize.

In today's marketplace, AI's use extends beyond just sorting and organizing. At Fullpath, we are most publicly using it within our platform to help customers find their answers, but we also leverage AI to supply talking points to sales people, perform vehicle comparisons for shoppers, execute A/B tests on ads, allocate and optimize budgets, build and suppress advertising audiences, and monitor, correct, and suggest improvements for ad copy and placement among other things.

Chapter 7: The Last(ing) Dealership

THINK BACK TO EVERYTHING WE'VE DISCUSSED IN THE LAST few chapters. Now, think ahead to the dealership of 2047.

What might look different if dealers spend the next 20+ years becoming technologically driven data-moguls? What would the customer experience look like? What might your team's day-to-day look like?

We see it like this:

Dealers will be wielding efficient, customer-centric, and nimble technology that, combined with their domain expertise and community positioning, enables them to outsmart and out perform anyone who comes up that is unique and special to tens of millions of working people around the world.

We are fully committed to continued innovation and are along for the ride, wherever it may take us. Over the last few years, we have continued to develop and pursue excellence and innovation in our products to better support our clients in achieving their goals - and that will always remain our central focus.

We believe deeply in the impact and importance of the great North American dealership, so much so that we have staked the entirety of our company on it. We believe that, with the right technologies and the right attitude, dealerships can prevail, with the industry's proverbial David beating out its Goliath, and hold on to the powerful economic and societal benefit that comes from something as seemingly simple as buying and selling a car.

LET'S CONTINUE THE CONVERSATION.

THANK YOU FOR READING OUR BOOK!

As people who are always working to learn more from those who know more, we are interested in hearing your thoughts and in receiving feedback on this book from the dealership community. Please feel free to reach out to us directly on LinkedIn or to send us an email so we can continue the conversation.

If you are interested in booking a demo of Fullpath's enhanced CDP, please reach out to the Fullpath team at get.started@fullpath.com.

Aharon Horwitz aharon@fullpath.com

Yishai Goldstein yishai@fullpath.com

Eliav Moshe eliav@fullpath.com

ABOUT THE AUTHORS

AHARON HORWITZ

Aharon Horwitz, CEO and co-founder of Fullpath, who hails from Cleveland, Ohio, grew up a diehard Cleveland Browns fan and holds an honors degree in Political Science from Columbia University. In 2007, Aharon co-founded PresenTense, a global incubator for socially minded startups, which established branches throughout the world, including in the US, Canada, Europe, and Israel. While leading PresenTense, Aharon became enamored with the impact that small and medium businesses can make on local economies. Teaming up with two technologically savvy friends from his army service and neighborhood, he launched the venture that would become Fullpath, which aims to deliver cutting-edge technology to car dealers, the quintessential family-owned, community-rooted business. As CEO of Fullpath, Aharon regularly speaks and writes about innovation. Aharon lives in Jerusalem with his wife Alieza and their two young children.

Eliav Moshe

Eliav Moshe, CPO and co-founder of Fullpath, was born and raised in Israel. He graduated from Hebrew University with a degree in Mathematics and has since become a top-rated application developer, an experienced lecturer in math and bioethical analysis, and a published author in multiple fields. His mobile applications have ranked #1 in key app-store categories, and he has decades of experience in applying analytics to software and user-acquisition growth. As Chief Product Officer at Fullpath, Eliav and his team have created the automotive industry's leading Customer Data Platform (CDP), marketing automation platform (MAP), and AI-backed sales enablement infrastructure. Eliav regularly writes and speaks about product development, customer journey applications, and the utilization of complex data acquisition environments in product development. Eliav lives in Jerusalem with his wife Leora and their four children.

YISHAI GOLDSTEIN

Yishai Goldstein, CTO and co-founder of Fullpath, is an expert in search technologies, natural language processing, data warehousing, and software development methodologies. His decades of experience in cutting-edge technologies underpins his role at Fullpath, where he focuses on scaling technology infrastructure, implementing new features, keeping client data secure, and maintaining a seamless and intuitive online system. In addition to being a software expert, Yishai enjoys working on complex mathematical and algorithmic techniques to support Fullpath's core product offering. Yishai holds a BSc. in Computer Engineering from the Hebrew University of Jerusalem. Prior to founding Fullpath, he built high-scale software infrastructure for Answers.com. Yishai loves kitchen gadgets and enjoys tasty food. Yishai lives in Jerusalem with his wife Suri and their three children.

ABOUT FULLPATH

Fullpath is the automotive industry's first enhanced Customer Data Platform (CDP). Fullpath unifies first-party dealership data and activates it by layering powerful AI and marketing automation on top to create a Customer Data and Experience Platform (CDXP). Dealerships that invest in the platform create exceptional, hyper-personalized customer experiences that drive loyalty and build resilient, lasting business.

fullpath

and the broader Riverwood team of analysts who so graciously give us their time every month.

Thank you to the whole Fullpath team, many of whom have been fellow travelers for longer than we ever imagined when we kicked this off in Yishai's living room way back when – and we couldn't be more grateful for it.

Thank you to our dear customers, so many of whom have been our teachers and guides along our path.

And finally, and most elementally, to our families, and especially our spouses, who have co-created this venture in every way.